Recollections of an Old Soldier

Autobiography of Captain David Perry, a Soldier of the United States' War of Independence

(American Revolutionary War History)

By David Perry

PANTIANOS
CLASSICS

Published by Pantianos Classics

ISBN-13: 978-1-78987-166-1

First published in 1822

Contents

District of Vermont

TO WIT:

Be it remembered, That on the third [22nd] day of February, in the forty-sixth year of the Independence of the United States of America, David Perry, of the said District, hath deposited in this office the title of a book, the right whereof he claims as proprietor, in the words following, to wit: "Recollections of an Old Soldier. The Life of Captain David Perry, a Soldier of the French and Revolutionary Wars. Containing many extraordinary occurrences relating to his own private history, and an account of some interesting events in the history of the times in which he lived, nowhere else recorded. Written by himself."

In conformity to the act of the Congress of the United States, entitled, "An act for the encouragement of learning, by securing the copies of maps, charts, and books, to the authors and proprietors of such copies, during the times therein mentioned."

JESSE GOVE,
Clerk of the District of Vermont.

A true copy of record.
Examined and sealed by me.
J. GOVE, *Clerk.*

Advertisement

IT was on a "cold wintry day," that the writer of the following Narrative called at the Printing Office -- it was a winter's day indeed, to most of his compatriots in the scenes of privations and blood-shed through which he had passed -- that the hoary-headed veteran of four score, called on the Printer, and made known his errand -- He was anxious to tell his tale of toils and hardships to his posterity, but, alas! pinching poverty, the too constant companion of patriotism and worth, had deprived him of the means. He had spent many days of his old age, in noting down, as the only legacy he could bequeath his posterity, the leading incidents of his life, and of the momentous times through which he had passed, which could avail them nothing, without the aid of *Printing,* "the art and preserver of all arts." Too poor to bear the expense himself, he solicited the Printer's assistance -- and who could withstand the solicitations of a war-worn Soldier of the Revolution, whose tale bears the impress of simplicity and truth, while it evinces no ordinary degree of devotion to the cause of liberty and his country? It was not in the Printer to do it; and he now looks to a liberal public for some trifling remuneration of his labor and expense, from the sale of this little volume.

Thousands, no doubt, of the Revolutionary Heroes, might have left a more brilliant specimen of talent and learning -- many have moved in a higher sphere of action, who have left no record of their toils and privations behind them -- but we venture to assert, that few have better earned the appellation of a *faithful Soldier,* than the subject of these memoirs. Though his name may not live on the annals of his country, yet his fellow-citizens should never forget, nor act unworthily of the sentiments of gratitude, which a recollection of this important truth should ever inspire, that, had it not been for the prowess and achievements -- the fortitude, patience and perseverance of those who, like himself, in the humbler ranks of the *common soldier*, bared their breasts to the foe, upon the "tented field," *that country* had never known "a name and a rank among the nations."

The profits of this work (if any) shall be reserved to defray the expenses of printing memoirs of other Revolutionary Soldiers, who may be in "reduced circumstances," should any such wish to avail themselves of the same for that purpose.

Part One – Formative Years

Chapter One – Childhood – 1741-1757

I was born August 8th, (O.S.) 1741 in the town of Rehoboth, Mass. I was the oldest child of Eliakim and Sarah Perry. The first thing of consequence that occurs to my mind, was the transactions relating to the war between the English and French. An army was raised in the New-England States, to go against Cape Breton, under Gen. Pepperell, at which time I was in my fifth year. My father and one of his brothers, and also one of my mother's brothers, enlisted into this army. And what strengthens my memory with regard to these events, one of my uncles above mentioned, whose name was Abner Perry, was killed at the taking of the Island Battery.

Nothing of consequence took place until the fall after I was seven years old, when my mother died, leaving four small children, viz: one brother and two sisters. There was something very singular took place respecting her sickness. She went with my father, to visit his relations at Eastown. They rode on horse-back. While they were there, on Lord's day, I was at play with my brother and two little sisters, and it appeared to me that I saw my mother ride by on the same horse she rode away on, and dressed in the same clothes. I mentioned the circumstance to my brother and sisters at the time; but she rode out of my sight immediately. At this time she was taken sick at Easton, in which condition they brought her home; and she died a few days afterwards. In consequence of this event, my father broke up house-keeping, [and put out his children]. Myself and sisters went to live with our uncle David Joy, the brother of my mother who, as I before said, went with my father to Cape Breton. I lived with my uncle (who treated me very kindly), until my fifteenth year; when I was placed with Mr. David Walker, in Dighton, Mass., to learn the trade of tanner and shoe-maker.

About this time war again broke out between the English and French, and it raged sorely in our part of the country, especially near the lakes. Our people made a stand at the south end of Lake George, where they built a fort, and another about 14 miles below, on the Hudson River, called Fort Edward. In 1755, a bloody battle was fought at the half-way-house, between Fort Edward and Lake George. Gen. Johnson commanded the English forces; and under him Maj. Rodgers commanded the Rangers. They had a number of sore battles with the French and Indians, and lost a great many of our best men. In the year 1757, Gen. Mont Calm came against Fort George, with a large army of French and Indians, and obliged the garrison to surrender; after which, contrary to his express agreement, he let loose his Indians upon our men, and massacred a great many of them.

Chapter Two – Ticonderoga – 1758

This year, in August, I was sixteen years old; at which age the young lads of that day were called into the training-bands. In the Spring of 1758, I was warned to training, and there were recruiting officers on the parade-ground, to enlist men for the next campaign. I enlisted into Capt. Job Winslow's company, of Col. Prebble's regiment, to serve eight months.-- People said I would not "pass muster," as I was small of my age; but there was no difficulty about that. When the company was full, we marched first to Worcester, staid there a few days, and then marched to Old Hadley. We remained here about a week. From this place we crossed the river to Northampton, where we drew five days' provisions -- left the place in the afternoon, and encamped a few miles out of town, in the woods for the night. - In that day there were no human habitations from

8

Northampton, to within ten miles of Albany. There was a small picket Fort in what was then called Pantocet Woods, commanded by Col. Williams. We had no other road than marked trees to direct our course -- no bridges on which to cross the streams; some of which we waded; others we passed on trees felled by our men: and for five successive nights we lay on the ground. We arrived at Greenbush, and, after a few days' tarry, marched up the North River to a place called Setackuk, where the Indians had driven off, captured, or destroyed the inhabitants. We here took a number of horses to draw the cannon to Lake George, but not having horses enough, some of the cannon were drawn by men. Part of the men went in Batteaus with the provisions. When we arrived at the Lake, the army, consisting of British and Americans, amounted to about 20,000 men. It was commanded by Gen. Abrecombe, and Lord Howe was second in command. We encamped there until boats and provisions enough were collected to carry us across the Lake, with cannon, &c. to attack Ticonderoga. We arrived at the Narrows the second morning after our embarkation, where we expected to be attacked by the enemy.

Major Rodgers, with his Rangers was the first to land. He was joined by Lord Howe and his party; and we had proceeded but a short distance into the woods, before we were met by the enemy, and a brisk fire ensued. It was the first engagement I had ever seen, and the whistling of balls, and roar of musketry terrified me not a little. At length our regiment formed among the trees, behind which the men kept stepping from their ranks for shelter. Col. Prebble, who, I well remember, was a harsh man, swore he would knock the first man down who should step out of his ranks; which greatly surprised me, to think that I must stand still to be shot at. Pretty soon, however, they brought along some wounded Frenchmen; and when I came to see the blood run so freely, it put new life into me. The battle proved a sore one for us. Lord Howe and a number of other good men, were killed.

The army moved on that day to within a short distance of the enemy, and encamped for the night. In the morning we had orders to move forward again, in a column three deep, in order to storm the enemy's breast-works, known in this country by the name of "the Old French Lines." Our orders were to "run to the breast-work, and get in if we could." But their lines were full, and they killed our men so fast, that we could not gain it. We got behind trees, logs and stumps, and covered ourselves as we could from the enemy's fire. The ground was strewed with the dead and dying. It happened that I got behind a white-oak stump, which was so small that I had to lay on my side, and stretch myself; the balls striking the ground within a hand's breadth of me every moment, and I could hear the men screaming, and see them dying all around me. I lay there some time. A man could not stand erect, without being hit, any more than he could stand out in a shower, without having drops of rain fall upon him; for the balls came by hands-full. It was a clear day -- a little air stirring. Once in a while the enemy would cease firing a minute or two, to have the smoke clear away, so that they might take better aim. In one of these intervals I sprang from my perilous situation, and gained a stand which I thought would be more secure, behind a large pine log, where several of my comrades had already taken shelter: but the balls came here as thick as ever. One of the men raised his head a little above the log, and a ball struck him in the centre of the forehead, and tore up his scalp clear back to the crown. He darted back, and the blood ran merrily; and, rubbing his face, said it was a bad blow, and no one was disposed to deny it, for he looked bad enough. We lay there till near sunset; and, not receiving orders from any officer, the men crept off, leaving all the dead, and most of the wounded. We had two of our company killed, and a number wounded. Our captain (Winslow) received a ball in his wrist, which passed up the fleshy part of his arm, and he carried it there as long as he lived, which was a number of years: he was afterwards raised to the rank of Colonel. Our Lieutenant was wounded by a shot in the leg, and one of our

Sargeants received a ball in his arm, which he carried with him to his grave.

We got away the wounded of our company; but left a great many crying for help, which we were unable to afford them. I suppose, that as soon as we left the ground, the enemy let loose his Indians upon them: for none of those that we left behind were ever heard of afterwards. We started back to our boats without any orders, and pushed out on the Lake for the night. We left between 6 and 7000, in killed and wounded, on the field of battle, which I believe is a greater number than ever was lost on our side, in one day, in all the battles that have been fought in America. We went over the Lake with about 21,000 men, in high spirits, with all kinds of music; but returned back melancholy and still, as from a funeral, and took our old stand at the south end of the Lake.

A great deal was said by the subaltern officers and men, at that time, with regard to the conduct of the commanding General. I was but a boy, and could have but little judgment about it then; but, from later experience and reflection, I think it looks more like the conduct of a Hull, a Wilkinson, or a Hampton, than like that of an able General and firm Patriot. We had artillery enough, and might have erected batteries; and it seems as though we might have taken the place. But it was thought by some, that the misfortune happened in consequence of the death of Lord Howe, as he was a more experienced officer.

Nothing of material consequence took place after this, for some time. Hardly a day passed, however, while we lay in camp, in which British and Yorkers did not flog some of their men. We were employed in building a fort.

Not long after, Major Rodgers and Major (afterwards General) Putnam, took charge of a party of men, on an expedition to a place called South Bay, where they met the enemy, and had a smart engagement. Maj. Putnam was taken and carried to Canada; and Maj. Rodgers returned to Fort Edward with what men they had left. While lying in camp, our water and provisions were very bad, the men grew sickly, and a great many died of the Dysentery. But the same Almighty Power that warded off the balls in the day of battle, preserved me from the desolating scourge of disease.

Towards Fall, Maj. Rodgers, with a party of men, went away to the westward, to a place called Cataraqua, and destroyed it.

It was during the Summer of this year, that Generals Wolfe and Amherst came from England with a fleet and army, and took Cape Breton; after which Gen. Amherst came and took command of our army, and Abrecombe went off.

When our times were out, we were dismissed, and went home. Our route was back to Albany, through Sharon and the "Green Woods," and over Glascow Mountain to Springfield, and so on to Worcester. I returned to my master, and went to work at my trade.

Chapter Three – Quebec – 1759

In the Spring of 1759, I enlisted under Lieut. John Richmond, expected to join Capt. Nathan Hogers' [Hodge's] company, with the lads that enlisted with me; but when we arrived at Worcester, Lieut. Richmond was transferred to Capt. Samuel Peck's company, of Boston. He (Lt. R.) urged me to go with him, as waiter, and told me I should live as well as he did. But Capt. Hogers said I should not go with him, and they contended pretty hard about it, till at last Maj. Caleb Willard, who had the command there, said it should be left to the lad's choice. I went with the Lieutenant, and he was as good as his word to my fare. We started for Boston: I rode his horse as much as he did until we gained the company. I never saw the Captain before, nor any of the company: but he proved to be a fine man, as was the first Lieutenant, whose name was Abbot. But the Ensign, (Larkin) was an Irishman and the company was a pretty rough set: I did not like them much.

This summer General Wolfe went up the River St. Lawrence with a fleet of about fifty men-of-war, and a great many transport ships.

We shipped a-board an English transport, under convoy of a frigate, and the first harbor we made was Cape Breton. The main fleet had sailed before we arrived. We lay there a few days, and sailed up the river after them, and, in forty-one days from the time we left Boston, we arrived at Quebec. Part of the main army had landed at Point Levi, and part on the other side of the river, below Mount Morancy Falls. We were landed on the Island of Orleans. On our first landing, considerable fighting took place, and many of the Rangers were killed. Two companies, one commanded by Capt. Danks, who was badly wounded, and the other by Captain Hazen, lost so many of their men, that they were put together, and did not then make a full company. They were stationed on that side of the river with General Wolfe: and they came to the Island to see if some of the provincials would go into their company. I turned out for one, and went into Capt. Hazen's company, and went ashore with them, and never saw my company again till after the city was taken, and we had got aboard the ship to return home.

We now had hard fighting enough, as we were scouting over the country nearly all the time, and were shot upon, more or less, nearly every day, and very often had some killed or wounded. We used frequently to get on board large flat-bottomed boats, that would hold eighty men each; to do which we had to wade in the water up to the middle; and, after sitting in our wet clothes all night, jump into the water again, wade ashore, go back into the woods, and scatter into small parties, in order to catch the inhabitants, as they returned from the woods to look after their domestic affairs; and when they had got in among us, one party would rise in their front, and another in their rear, and thus we surrounded and captured a great many of them.

The country was settled on that side of the river, to the distance of about thirty miles below our encampment; and we took the greater part of their cattle and sheep, and drove them into camp. We went down there a number of times, and found that they had a considerable force stationed back in the woods. One night in particular, I well remember, our company and a company of regulars, took a trip down there in boats, and landed about day-break. As soon as it was light, Capt. Hazen told his men to stroll back, a few at a time, undiscovered, into the woods. As soon as we had done this, the regulars marched, by fife and drum, in a body round a point of the woods, in order to draw the enemy there; and we kept still, until they got between us and the regulars, when we rose and fired on them, and put them to flight immediately. Our orders were, to "kill all, and give no quarters." The enemy had a Priest with them, who was wounded in the thigh, and begged earnestly for *quarters:* but the Captain told the men to kill him. Upon which, one of them deliberately blew his brains out. -- We effectually broke up the camp in this quarter, and returned safe to camp.

At another time, we went down the river about forty miles, in the night, and landed in the morning on the opposite side to the place last mentioned, and secreted ourselves in small parties, in the woods, beside the road. I was with the Lieutenant's party. We had a man by the name of Frazier in our party, who enlisted under Capt. Peck, in Boston, and he was a pretty unruly fellow. There came along three armed Frenchmen near where we lay concealed, and Frazier saw them, and hallooed to them *"boon-quarter;"* whereupon one of them levelled his piece and shot him through the head, and killed him instantly. The Captain hearing the report, came and inquired how it happened. We told him we could not keep Frazier still; "well," said he, "his blood be upon his own head." We now expected to have some fighting. We left our blankets upon the dead man, and took the road the Frenchmen came in, and after marching about half a mile, we came into an open field, with a large number of cattle in it: and on the opposite side of the field, just in the edge of the woods, were a great many little huts, full of women and children, with their hasty-pudding for breakfast, of which I partook with them; but their little children scampered into the brush, and could not be got sight of again, any more than so many [young] partridges. We did not, however, wish to hurt them. There were three

14

barns in the lot, filled with household goods: we took as many as we could of these, and drove the cattle back the way we came, to where the dead man and blankets were left, which we took up, and were proceeding with our booty to the river, when the enemy fired on us, and killed Lieut. Meachum, of Capt. Dank's company, and wounded one other. In the mean time, the cattle we had taken all ran back; but we drove off the enemy, and got our goods, &c., aboard the boats, and returned to camp.

About this time the French fixed long fire rafts on the banks of the river, near the lower town, and filled them with fuel, and other combustible materials. Our shipping lay below, to the number of about three hundred sail, and nearly filled the river: and in the night, when the wind and tide favored their project, they communicated fire to this raft, and set it afloat down the river. It was nearly half a mile in length, and so rapidly did the flames extend from one end of it to the other, that it seemed as though the whole river was on fire. The men-of-war despatched their boats with iron hooks and grapples, and fastened one end of it, and so turned it endwise. Some of the vessels, in the meantime, weighed anchor -- others cut their cables; and in this way they opened a passage, and towed this threatening engine of destruction through the fleet, without sustaining much damage.

That part of the army stationed on Point Levi had batteries erected, and threw shells, and shot from them into the town all the time, and burnt and demolished a great many of their buildings. On the side of the river, where we lay, a large river, which has its rise in the mountains, empties into the St. Lawrence against the Morancy Falls. This river was not fordable back to the mountain; but below the falls, when the tide was out, it spread over the marsh, and was so shallow that men could wade in it. The banks of the St. Lawrence are very high, and the French built a strong breast-work on them, to prevent Gen. Wolfe getting to the city that way. And we had a battery against them on the opposite side of the above-mentioned river, from which we kept up a pretty constant fire at each other for a long time, but without much effect on either party. At length Gen. Wolfe ordered a couple of ships up against their breast-work, at high water, with cannon on board, and anchored them, with springs on their cables, in a position to fire on, and with intent to batter down the enemy's works; but when the tide fell, the vessels grounded, and the crews relinquished the project, set them on fire, and returned in their boats.

Soon after this, at low water, General Wolfe ordered his men to pass down the banks, and cross the river by platoons, in order to storm their breast-work. They formed in solid column, as they reached the opposite shore, to the number of about two thousand. The enemy did not fire a single shot until our men had formed, when they opened upon them the most destructive fire I ever witnessed: it appeared to me that nearly four-fifths of them fell at the first discharge, and those who did not fall turned about promiscuously and came back without any order. Our company remained on the bank, with our muskets loaded, as a kind of corps de reserve, to follow the detachment, in case it succeeded in making a breach in the enemy's works. Gen. Wolfe stood with us, where we could see the whole maneuver; and the tide came and swept them off together. -- And there arose the most tremendous thunder-shower I ever witnessed; which, combined with the continual roar of cannon and musketry conspired to produce a truly sublime and awful scene!

Gen. Wolfe then broke up his encampment on that side of river, and went over to Point Levi. A few nights after, Capt. Warren, commander of a sixty-four man-of-war, was ordered to pass by the town, up the river; and, wind and tide favoring, he went by, under the most tremendous cannonade I ever heard, and we expected she would be blown to atoms, but never a shot hit her. A few nights afterwards two more vessels passed up, under similar circumstances, and had their rigging considerably cut to pieces.

The country this side the river was settled to the distance of about one hundred and sixty miles below. All the rangers, and one company of Light-Infantry of the British, were ordered to go a-board vessels, and to sail down the river as far as it was settled, then to land and march back towards the City, burning and destroying, in our course, all their buildings, killing all their cattle, sheep and horses, and laying waste the country far and near.

The company to which I belonged, landed early one morning, and we went directly to a large house, about a quarter of a mile distant. The people fled at our approach, and we caught plenty of pigs, geese, and fowls; and while part of our men were busied in carrying the squawling and squealing booty to the vessels, there came a Frenchman out of the woods, and ran into the house. We followed after and took him, and carried him a-board the vessels. And the officers told him if he would be friendly to us, and pilot us to their back settlements, he should be used well; which he complied with, and he proved true to his engagements. Having breakfasted a-board the ship, our whole party went up to the house just mentioned, where we found large stores of provisions, of one kind and another, and among the rest a plenty of pickled Salmon, which was quite a rarity to most of us; and as we had been several days a-board the vessels, we concluded to stay there the day and night, and went to cooking Salmon for dinner, &c. The men strolled about as they pleased, and pretty soon we heard three or four guns fired a short distance from us, and we paraded immediately, to see who was missing. It appeared there were only two absent, viz: Lieut. Toot, of Capt. Stark's [1] company, and a private. We then marched to the place from which the report had been heard, and found the soldier, who had been shot and scalped, who died soon after. The Lieutenant returned unhurt. We marched on a little distance, and came to a large opening. Here we surrounded and took a Frenchman, from whom we endeavored to learn what had become of those who fired the guns, but he would not tell; and the Captain told him he would kill him if he did not, at the same time directing us to draw our knives, upon our doing which he fell to saying his prayers upon his knees, firmly refusing to tell. Finding him thus resolute and faithful to his friends, the Captain sent him a prisoner to the shipping, and we went to our cooking again.

In the morning our company took the friendly Frenchman for a guide, and marched off three or four miles to a back village, and got there before it was light. We were divided into small parties, as usual, in order to take what prisoners we could. I was stationed in a barn with the Lieutenant's party, and while we lay there, a Frenchman came along smoking his pipe, and one of our men, an *outlandish* sort of a fellow, put his gun out of a crack in the barn, and, before we had time to prevent it, fired upon the man; the shot carried away his pipe, but did him no other injury, and he ran off. But when the Captain heard of it, he flogged the soldier severely. We burnt the buildings, destroyed everything there, and returned towards the river again. The main party marched up the river, burning and destroying everything before them: and our company followed on some distance in the rear, collecting the cattle, sheep and horses, and burning the scattering buildings, &c. In this way we continued our march at the rate of about twelve miles a day. Every six miles we found large stone churches, at one of which we generally halted to dinner, and at the next to supper, and so on. We lived well, but our duty was hard -- climbing over hills and fences all day; always starting in the morning before break of day, in order to make prisoners of some of the enemy, in which we were hardly ever disappointed. We were very often fired on by the enemy, and many of our men were killed or wounded, in these excursions. Where there was a stream to cross, in our course, they would take up the bridge, secrete themselves on the opposite side and fire on us unawares.

Our Captain was a bold man. I have seen him cock his piece, and walk promptly up to the enemy, face to face; and our men would never shrink from following such an officer, and they seldom followed him without success.

While we were on this tour, Gen. Wolfe landed his main army on the Plains of Abraham; Gen. Mont Calm sallied forth from the City, and a battle took place, the result of which is well known: both the commanding Generals were killed, the second in command on the side of the British badly wounded, with the loss of a great many men, on both sides; but the English remained masters of the field.

And we continued our route up the river till we had proceeded about sixty miles, when a vessel came down from the main army, with information of the battle and victory, and with orders for us to "drive on faster, and destroy all before us." We continued our march three days more, which brought us to within about sixty miles of head-quarters, when a second vessel came down to us, with orders to cease burning and pillaging, for Quebec had given up to the English. We went a-board our vessels, and sailed up to the city, and landed at the lower town, where we witnessed the destruction made there. From the lower, we went to the upper town, up their dug-way; and it was truly surprising to see the damage done to the buildings, &c. by the shot and shells that were thrown into the town by our artillery. Their houses were principally made of stone and lime -- the gable-ends of wood, which were burnt out of a great many of them, and cannon balls stove holes through the buildings in many places, [and a great number drove the stones part way out,] and remained in the walls. The city surrendered to Brigadier General Townsend, as Major General Wolfe was killed, and General Monkton badly wounded. We were sent up the river about four miles above the city, as a vessel guard.

Nothing of consequence took place after this, till our times were out, when we were sent back to our company, a-board ship, to return home. The ship's crew were very sickly, having lain still all Summer on the Island. -- Lieut. Richmond, with whom I enlisted, was very sick, as also were a great many of the soldiers between decks, and I had to take care of them. Lieut. Richmond kept sending for me to attend on him, and I grew tired of it, and refused to go; upon which Capt. Peck sent for me, to know why I would not, and I told him it was as much as I could do to take care of the sick privates. He then told me to come and live in the cabin, and wait upon Lieut. Richmond, which should be my duty, and I did so.

Owing to bad weather, we were a long time getting down the river, and before we arrived at Halifax eight or nine of our men died and were thrown overboard. When we arrived at Halifax, I went ashore, and found my old Captain (Winslow) there, who had been promoted to the rank of Major. He wished me to stay and go home with him before Spring, and I did as he desired, and lived with him and the Colonel of the regiment, till about the first of February, when we set sail for Boston, and had a long passage of twenty-one days. On our passage we made the harbors of Penobscot, Portsmouth, and Cohasset, at which last place I left the vessel, and went home on foot.

[1] This is Gen. John Stark, who is now living at Pembroke, N. Hampshire; and, according to my best recollection as to his age, he is rising of 95 years old. I have frequently been told, within a few years, by intelligent persons, that Gen. S. and myself are the only men now living in New-England, who belonged to the army which took Quebec.

Chapter Four - Nova Scotia - 1760-61

This year [1759] Gen. Amherst went over the lake with an army, where we went the year preceding, and took Crown-Point and Ti-conderoga, with the loss of but few men: and in the fall he went back to Albany with his main army, leaving a sufficient force to garrison the places he had taken. In the Spring of 1760, he went up to the head of Mohawk river, and from thence proceeded to Wood-Creek, and on through the western waters to Lake Ontario, and thence down the river St. Lawrence to Montreal, which town surrendered to him without much resistance, and thus terminated the war in that quarter.

After I had been at home about a month, Major Winslow told me, that if I would enlist what men I could, and go back to Halifax with him, I should have a sergeant's berth, as soon as there was a vacancy for one in any of the companies; and if no vacancy occurred, I should be cleared from duty through the season. I accordingly enlisted eight or ten likely young men, and went on with them to Boston. There being no vessel ready at the time we arrived at Boston, we were billetted out at the house of a widow, named Mosely; and while we were here the town took fire in the night. -- It originated in a tavern, (sign of the Gold Ball) in Main or King's Street, at about midnight, the wind in the north-west and pretty high; and in spite of all we could do with the engines, &c. it spread a great way down King's Street, and went across and laid all that part of the town in ashes, down to Fort Hill. We attended through the whole, and assisted in carrying water to the engines. The number of buildings burnt was about three hundred.

As soon as the vessel was ready, we sailed for Halifax, and arrived there in four days. -- There being no vacancy for a sergeant's berth, I lived with the Colonel, Major and Chaplain of the regiment, and fared very well.

During the Summer some of the Connecticut people obtained a grant of a number of towns in the Menus country and moved on to settle them; and as there were a considerable number of French and Indians in that quarter, they wanted a guard to protect them. A draft was made from our regiment, to obtain men for that purpose. I wanted to see that country, and turned out for one of the detachment. Just previous to our departure, a man and woman were executed for murder -- the woman killed a small girl that was living with her.

We set out from Halifax by water, and went to the head of the Bason to fort Sackfield, about twelve miles distant; from that place we went by land about thirty miles through the woods, and then came into a fine open country. There was a fort here, called Fort Pisga, with a considerable number of troops in it. Beside this fort ran a large river, of the same name, (Pisga River) over which we passed in boats, into the Menus country. The people had laid out two

21

towns, one called Horton, and the other Cornwallis. We were stationed at the latter, it being the farthest from Fort Pisga. We had a very agreeable time of it, among our own country people, and built a picket fort there; but there was not much need of it, for the French and Indians were quite peaceable, and to all appearance friendly. At one time about thirty of the Indians, with their Sachem, came to see us. I talked with the Sachem some time; and, among other things, about going a hunting with him. I asked him if he would use me well: he said, if I did as he bid me, he would; if not, that he would kill me. On such terms, I thought it best not to try a new master. Two French families came to reside with us, who were very friendly and useful to our people, and learned them many useful arts, and among others, how to catch fish, which was of great service to them, as the provisions they brought with them were soon exhausted. But as they could not subsist *on fish alone*, many of them must in all probability have starved, if we had not dealt out to them provisions from the king's stores.

Three large rivers run through the town of Cornwallis. At high water vessels of the largest size could sail up and down them with safety. These rivers made a vast quantity of marshy land, and the upland between them was not very good. I did not like the country, but staid there till our times were out, and then returned to Halifax, where we remained till a transport could be provided, when about one hundred and fifty of us shipped aboard a large British Snow, for Boston, and we had fine weather for a few days; but while our top-sails, &c. were all standing, and every thing indicated a short and prosperous voyage, there came on a sudden squall of wind, and stripped our sails all to pieces. The seas ran mountain high, and every soul of us momently expected to go to the bottom. The Captain of the vessel said he had followed the seas fifteen years, and never experienced such a gale before. But being a good new-built vessel, she rode out the storm, which lasted several days, and blowed us so far out of our course that we were obliged to be put on short allowance, of one sea-biscuit and a half, each, per day; or in lieu of the biscuit, a piece of butter of the size of a hen's egg -- or a slice of beef as large as one's three fingers. We lived on this allowance about a fortnight, when we arrived at Boston. I went home to my master, to work at my trade again.

This completed the third campaign in which I had served as a private: and I do not remember that in all this time I was ever so unwell as to lose a meal of victuals, or to miss a tour of duty: and I think I have the greatest reason to bless and praise the name of the Lord, that he covered my head in the day of battle, and preserved my body from wasting sickness at noon-day.

Chapter Five – Newfoundland – 1761-1762

I worked at my trade this year -- the war in our part of the country being pretty much over, a few soldiers only being retained for garrison duty.

In 1762, the state raised a regiment of men to go to Halifax. It was commanded by Col. Jonathan Hoar, and Maj. Winslow was Lieut. Colonel under him. As there was no recruiting officer near him, Col. Winslow persuaded me to enlist once more into the service. I had orders to enlist what men I could; and having obtained a number of recruits, I proceeded with them to join the Regiment at the Castle, near Boston, and was directed to enter Capt. Abel Cain's [Keen's] company. Here I was appointed a sergeant. We shipped for Halifax, arrived there without any occurrence of note, and encamped a little out of the town, in tents. We were employed in wheeling off the top of *Citadel Hill*, so called, in order to erect a fort upon it. Our duty was pretty hard, but then we worked without any apprehensions of being fired upon by an enemy.

There is one thing I would here notice, which shows a specimen of British cruelty without a parallel, I could hope, in the history of that nation. Three men, for some trifling offence which I do not recollect, were tied up to be whipped. One of them was to receive eight hundred lashes, the others five hundred apiece. By the time they had received three hundred lashes, the flesh appeared to be entirely whipped from their shoulders, and they hung as mute and motionless as though they had been long since deprived of life. But this was not enough. The doctor stood by with a vial of sharp stuff, which he would ever and anon apply to their [noses, and finding, by the pain it gave] them, that some signs of life remained, he would tell them, "d--mn you, you can bear it yet" -- and then the whipping would commence again. It was the most cruel punishment I ever saw inflicted, or had ever conceived of before -- by far worse than death. I felt at the time as though I could have taken summary vengeance on those who were the authors of it, on the spot, had it been in my power to do it.

During this year an expedition was fitted out by the English, and American Colonies, against the Havanna, which they succeeded in taking.

In the course of the Summer, the French came and took New-foundland. In a town called St. Johns, was a very strong fort, built with stone and lime, at the head of the harbor. The French took possession of this fort, and distressed the inhabitants very much. After it was ascertained how strong they were by land and by sea, the commander of the British land forces, Col. [William] Amherst, (brother to Gen. [Jeffrey] Amherst) and Lord Caldwell [Colvill], commander of the fleet, held a council of war on board the commander's ship. The result of the consultation was, that we had a force sufficient to go and re-take the place, and accordingly immediate preparations were made. It was necessary there should be a company selected out of our regiment for Rangers, of which Capt. William Barron was appointed commander; and as I had become somewhat familiar with a sergeant's duty, he requested me to go into his company, and I complied. When all things were ready, we set sail with three ships of the line, two or three frigates, and about two thousand five hundred soldiers, British and Americans. We had a good passage. The enemy having possession of the Harbor, we could not make the land in that direction, but were compelled to sail round a few miles to Tarpolin Cove, [Torbay Bight] where we landed, though not without much difficulty -- the wind blowing strong, and the seas ran so high, that the ships dragged their anchors. But we at length succeeded in landing all our men &c. and marched several miles through the woods, till we came within sight of the fort. They fired on us with their cannon, but we lay behind the rocks, [so that they could do us no harm. It was a fair day. I walked out alone from behind the rocks,] and saw the men in the fort about firing a cannon in the direction in which I stood. I had heard it remarked that a ball could be seen in the air after it left the cannon's mouth, and thought this a good time to ascertain the truth of what appeared so incredible to me. I stood my ground. The piece was fired, and before the ball got half way to me, I could see where it was, by its driving the air together, and forming a blue kind of substance about the size of a barrel.

There were two very high hills near the harbor of St. Johns; one was called Flagstaff-Hill, and the other Gibbet-Hill. The enemy had possession of both. These hills commanded the ground on which it was desirable to erect our Batteries, to play on the fort. On [the] Flagstaff-Hill the enemy had placed three hundred men, in a situation very difficult to be got at by an opposing force. After dark our company and a company of British Light Infantry, commanded by Capt. MacDonald [McDonnell], set out under the guidance of one of the inhabitants, and marched in an Indian file round the hill, until we were pretty near the enemy's sentinels. Here we sat down upon the ground, and remained all night without speaking a word, until day-break, when the word was whispered from the front to the rear, to march forward. We had a Frenchman in our company, and when we were hailed by the Sentinels, he would answer them in French, and by this means we succeeded in taking several of them, without alarming the main force at the top of the hill. But before we had reached the top, one of them fired on us, which gave notice of our approach to their van guard, who immediately opened a brisk fire upon our foremost men. We however rushed on till we came near their main party. In the mean time, Capt. MacDonald was so badly wounded that he died soon after, and about thirty of our party were either killed or wounded. We killed and took about the same number of the enemy. The Lieutenant of the British company and myself, were foremost, and we advanced on and found their stepping-place, and while running up it, the Lt. was shot through the vitals, and he died soon after. Thus I was all alone, the remainder of our party not having gained the summit; the enemy retreated, and I followed them to the other end of the hill. -- In my route on the hill, I picked up a good French gun, and brought it home with me.

It pretty soon commenced raining exceedingly hard, and continued to rain until about midnight of the next night, when it cleared away. We remained masters of the hill, and were obliged to remain on it without a mouthful of food or drink of any sort, until morning of the second day after we started, when a British Colonel came on the hill, and applauded us very highly for our exploit and success, and said we should have some refreshment. Gibbet-hill, before mentioned, was between us and the fort, and we could not tell whether there were any of the enemy's men on it or not. The British Col. told Capt. Barron to send two men to the top of this hill, and direct them to retreat if they found any body there, if they did not, to swing their hats. Capt. Barron turned immediately to me, and said "Sergeant Perry, take a man with you, and go to the top of the hill," and before I had time to pick one, he ordered Peter Laford, the Frenchman who deceived the Sentry on Flagstaff-hill, to go with me. After we had started, Peter said the Captain ought not to have sent him; for they would kill him if they took him. He said "we must throw the Priming out of our guns, and if they take us, we will tell them we deserted -- and we shall soon be re-taken." I told him he might throw *his* priming out if he chose, but I would not *mine.* The brush was so wet, however, that we could not have used our pieces, if we had occasion. We at length gained the top of the hill, and swung our hats as a signal that there was none of the enemy on it.

We could see into the enemy's fort, which was nearer to us than our men. They fired a cannon at us, the ball went over our heads, and struck on the other hill within six feet of our [own] men, who were all paraded, but did no injury. Pretty soon the Commander, with his men, came to Gibbet-Hill to look out a place for his battery, and set those of his men to work on the battery, who had not been engaged in taking Flagstaff-hill. Our company were much fatigued. -- The enemy kept up a constant fire upon us, and threw balls and shells on the hill, but did not make very great slaughter, though some of our men were killed. While a squad of regulars sat eating their breakfast in a tent, a cannon ball passed through it, and killed one man instantly; and another by the name of David Foster, belonging to Capt. Cain's company, was struck on the temple bone by a grape shot, which passed under his forehead, rolled his eyes out, and left a little piece of the lower part of his nose standing; and what I thought was very remarkable, he lived to get home -- but how much longer I do not know for a certainty; though, about ten years ago, I was credibly informed that he was [then] living in the State of Massachusetts.

We landed at the Island, on Monday morning -- on Tuesday morning took possession of Flagstaff-Hill, and on Wednesday broke up the ground for our batteries -- so that by Friday they were ready to open upon the enemy. At about 12 o'clock on Friday night, having eleven mortars fixed, we commenced throwing shells in great abundance, into the enemy's Fort, which caused much screaming and hallooing in their ranks, and did great execution. We kept them flying the remainder of the night, and until the sun was about two hours high on Saturday morning, when the enemy sent out a flag, with proposals for a capitulation. But the conditions were such as our commander could not agree to, and we went at it again as hard as ever, and so continued, till the sun was about two hours high at night. They then sent out another flag of truce, bringing word that

27

they had concluded to comply with the terms we offered them in the morning: and about sun-set they marched out of the fort, and we marched in, and took possession.

A few days after this, three men-of-war arrived at the harbor of St. Johns from Havana, for assistance, and bringing news of the surrender of that place to the English. There was great rejoicing in the fort and on board the vessels, on the occasion of these signal successes. We remained here a short time, and, having put all things to rights, we shipped for Halifax, leaving British soldiers enough to garrison the fort.

After being some time at sea, the men grew sickly, and on our way a great many were taken sick, and I was among the number. I had the nervous fever. When we arrived at Halifax, our times were out; but I was so unwell, that instead of returning home, I was obliged to go to the hospital. I told my friends that were discharged, as we parted, that they would never see me again, for I was very sick and out of my head -- and no one thought I could live long. I remained in the hospital some time, but was so deranged that I cannot tell exactly how long. I had my reason, however, by turns; and in one of these intervals, I remember perfectly well, Doctor Matthews, the surgeon of our regiment, had me brought into his room, and tried to make me drink some sour punch, but I told him I could not. He asked me if I did not love it when I was well. I told him I did. At another time I came to myself so much as to know that the body lice were eating me up, and told one of those who waited on me, to heat a tailor's goose which was in the room, and iron my blanket on both sides, which he did, and it turned it as red as blood.

Capt. Barron staid with us all winter, and the British gave him a Lieutenant's commission in the standing army, for his valor in taking Flagstaff-Hill at Newfoundland. He came to see me, and I told him I wanted to go home. He asked me if I would not have staid, if I had been well. I told him, no. He then said he would see that I was put a-board the first vessel that sailed for Boston. He asked me if I had any money. I told him I did not know what had become of my money or clothes; upon which he took from his pocket a cob dollar and gave it me, but what became of it I never knew. -- The Captain was as good as his word, for in a few days after I was put a-board a vessel for Boston. I do not know the name of the Captain, nor how long I was on the passage: but I remember they once took me up on deck, it being a very pleasant day, and combed my head, and my hair all rolled off.

While I was on board that vessel, it appears to me that I died -- that I went through the excruciating pains of the separating of soul and body, as completely as ever I shall again, (and such a separation must soon take place) and that I was immediately conveyed to the gate of Heaven, and was going to pass in; but was told by one, that I could not enter then, but in process of time, if I would behave as he directed, on the set time I should have admittance. It appeared to me that my feet stood on a firm foundation, and that I stood there for the space of about a half hour. In this time there appeared to be a continual flowing up of people, as we suppose they die; and none stopped, but all passed off, one way or the other. Just at my left hand, there appeared to be the opening of a great gulph, and the greater part of the grown people seemed to pass off there. Once in a while one passed through the gate into the Holy City. One person appeared, with whom I had been intimately acquainted, and it appeared to me that I knew him as well as ever I did: it was Doct. Matthews -- [and whether I saw him or not, he died, as I afterwards learned, while I was sick on board the ship]. The one that talked with me, told me about the Revolutionary War, and showed me the British vessels in the harbor of Boston, as plainly as I saw them when they came. And during the first year of that war, I was down there in Gen. Putnam's regiment, and I went on Roxbury hill to see the shipping in the harbor, and they looked exactly as they had been shown to me many years before. This transition (as I firmly believe) from life to death, and from death to life, which took place nearly sixty years ago, is as fresh in my mind now as it was then; and not many days have passed from that time to this, which have not brought the interesting scenes I then witnessed, clearly to view in my mind. But I never dared to say any thing about it, for a great many years afterwards, for fear of being ridiculed. But about the [last of February or first of January, 1763], peace was declared between England, France and Spain, and the people rejoiced exceedingly on account of it. I told them we should have another war soon. They asked me why I thought so. I told them the British had settled peace with their foreign enemies, but they could not long live in peace, and they would come against us next. But I never told my own wife, nor any other person, of what happened to me on board the vessel, as above related, for nearly thirty years afterwards, when a great deal was said in the neighborhood where I lived, about one Polly Doves, of Grantham, N.H., who was taken very sick, so that no one thought she could live long, and many times the people thought she was dying. In one of these turns she had a dream or vision, by which she was assured that, on a stated Sunday, she should be healed, and go to meeting the same day. On the Saturday night, previous to the time appointed, many people stood round her bed, expecting every moment that she would breathe her last: but when the hour she had mentioned arrived, she rose from her bed, and said she was well: and Captain Robert Scott carried her some distance to meeting, behind him on horseback, the same day she recovered. There was so much talk about it, that I ventured to tell my experience as before described, and have since told it to a great many people; and some believe it, and others do not.

But to return to my narrative. -- When we arrived in Boston harbor, the authority of the place would not permit the sick to be brought into town, for fear of the fever; and I was carried to the Castle. A Major Gay, who was there at the time, was very kind to me, and took me into his room, and gave me some refreshment. -- He asked me if I had any friends that would come and take care of me, if they knew I was there. I told him that I did not doubt but that my uncle David Joy would come, if he knew it; upon which he sat down and wrote him a letter, and despatched a boat a-shore, with

directions to leave it at Martin's tavern, where, it fortunately happened, was a man going directly to Rehoboth, who took the letter
and carried it to my uncle that very night. The second day after the
letter was written, my uncle arrived with a horse and chair, and
took me off by the way of Dorchester Point. When I got into the
chair, I felt nicely; and told my uncle, that if the horse could stand it,
I would ride home that night, a distance of forty-four miles. But
my resolution soon forsook me. I became extremely weak, and my
delirium returned, so that my uncle was unable to get me to a tavern. He carried me to a private house the first night, and it took him
three days more to get me home, where we arrived on the ninth
day of December, which was the day appointed by the civil authority for public Thanksgiving. -- I think I had the greatest reason to
give thanks to God, of any body in the world, for sparing my life in
so many trying scenes, and safely returning me to my friends again.

I remained sick at my uncle's house about two months, and my
recovery for most of that period, was considered doubtful; but in
process of time it pleased God to restore me to health.

Part Two - The Connecticut Years

Chapter Six - Killingly 1762-1775 - Marriage, Tanning and Shoemaking

In August this year, (1762) I was twenty-one years old. Before I went on the last tour in the Spring, I agreed with my master, and got up my indentures. As he had all my wages for the former campaigns, I thought I would have them this year myself; but by reason of sickness, &c. I spent or lost them, and all my clothes, except those I had on at the hospital.

In April, 1763, I left my native home, and went into the town of Killingly, Connecticut, and agreed to work for a man six months, at my trade. On the 12th of January, 1764, I was married; at which time I was not worth ten dollars, besides my clothes. I followed shoe-making, made a comfortable living by it, and soon was able to buy a few acres of land, upon which I erected tan-works -- had a pretty good run of custom, and the inhabitants assisted all they could. Thus for a time matters went on prosperously, and in three or four years I gained considerable property. But there was another tanner in Killingly, named Watson, who used to have all the custom before I set up business there, and had become pretty rich. Finding his custom decrease as mine gained, he came and proposed to take me into partnership with him, so that we could carry on the business on a large scale. I closed with him, and in three years he managed to get all I had earned, and left me two hundred dollars in debt.

Chapter Seven - Siege of Boston - 1775-1776

Fifth Campaign (First Campaign of the Revolution).
Rank: 2nd Lieutenant.

This brings me up to our Revolutionary War. In the Spring of 1775, as there could be no accommodation of the difficulties between Great Britain and the Americans, the British troops marched out of Boston to Lexington and Concord, and killed a number of our men, which aroused every part of the country to arms! An army was immediately raised, and I was appointed a Lieutenant in Capt. Fleet's [Joseph Elliot's] company, and General Putnam's regiment. As soon as our company was full, (and it did take long to fill it) the ensign and myself marched with it to Roxbury, and quartered our men in the Loring house. In a few days the Captain and the other Lieutenant joined us. The Captain, however, was soon taken sick, and died before he had done one tour of duty. We remained there until after the 17th of June, on which day the Bunker-Hill fight took place; but my company was not in it. This was a severe battle, especially to the British, who had 1053 killed and wounded, according to their returns, including a great proportion of officers. We had 78 killed, and 86 wounded, and among the slain was the noble Gen. Warren, whose death was a great loss to our army and country. Our regiment, immediately after this battle, was collected together on Prospect-Hill, where we built a fort. The British were in possession of Bunker-Hill, about three quarters of a mile distant, and in plain sight of our works.

This Spring Gen. Ethan Allen went and took Crown Point from the British, together with a number of cannon, which were of great service to us, as we had but a small quantity of artillery.

When the fort was completed on Prospect-Hill, our cannon were placed within point-blank shot of the enemy; and as I was walking one day with an old experienced officer, I asked him why he did not fire upon the enemy? He said, if, by our formidable appearance, we could keep them where they were, we should do well, for we had not ammunition enough to last one day and a half. There was but little fighting this season, except some small skirmishes between the sentinels of the out-posts, which were soon put a stop to.

In the heat of Summer, the men were attacked with the Dysentery, and considerable numbers of them died. The people flocked in from the country, to see the camps and their friends, and took the disorder; and it spread all over the New-England states: it carried off a great many more in the country than in the camp, which seemed to dishearten the people very much. But in the latter part of winter General Washington marched a considerable force on to Dorchester Point, in the night, erected temporary batteries, and conveyed his cannon to them -- and in the morning, when the British came to find their fleet exposed to his fire, they sent word to him, that if he fired on their shipping, they would burn the town: but if he would let them pass out of the harbor unmolested, they would quit the place; and they did so. -- Gen. Washington expected their next object would be New-York, and marched all his [troops immediately for that city. He] went by land, and arrived there before the enemy did by water: but, for want of men and ammunition, he was obliged to evacuate the city to them.

Chapter Eight - Winter in Providence, Rhode Island 1776-1777

Sixth Campaign (2nd Campaign of the Revolution).
Rank: 1st Lieutenant.

About this time several regiments were raised for one year's service. Col. Durgee, who commanded one of them, pressed me hard to take a Captain's commission in his regiment. But as I was poor at that time, and had a wife and five small children to support, or if I went, to leave without the proper means of support, I could not comply with his wishes. I told him a soldier ought not to have any thing to think of at home.

But they could not raise men enough, without making large drafts of militia. In the Fall of the year, a number of regiments were ordered to be raised for the winter. I had the appointment of a first Lieutenant, and was ordered to march with my company to New-York. We accordingly set out, and had proceeded one day, when I had counter orders, to go to Providence, the enemy having taken possession of Newport. I was put into Col. John Ely's regiment, which was under the command of Gen. Spencer, and remained at Providence till the expiration of the term for which we were called out, without any occurrence of importance, and then returned home.

Chapter Nine - The Home Front - 1777-1779

Poverty, and Efforts in Recruiting Men.

In the year 1777, Congress, and the states individually, made an attempt to raise an army for three years, or during the war, that Gen. Washington might have an army that he could depend upon: but it was difficult to raise such a force. The government of Connecticut passed a law providing, that if any two men would procure one soldier to enlist for three years or during the war, they should be exempted from a draft during that period. One of my neighbors wished me to find a man who would enlist, and he would pay one half, and find somebody to pay the other half. I found a man as he desired: but my neighbor failed to get a partner as he proposed, and the man refused to go, unless the whole sum was paid him in advance. I was so anxious to have the man enlisted, that, notwithstanding my poverty, I paid him twenty pounds myself, although I was not exposed to a draft. This settled the difficulty; and I afterwards enlisted several others.

Chapter Ten - Plainfield - 1779-1797

Selectman and Militia Service.
Rank: Captain.

As there is history extant giving account of the principal events of the whole war, I will confine myself merely to an account of my domestic concerns. Nothing material with regard to them took place, until the month of March, in the year 1779, when I left Connecticut, and moved into Plainfield, New Hampshire.

I lived in that town eighteen years. The inhabitants of this part of the country were not much distressed after I moved here; for Burgoyne was taken, and that pretty much stopped the enemy's progress to the northward, except a party that came and burnt Royalton (that being a frontier town in those days,) and went off again without much opposition.

Vermont was not at that time recognized as a state. New-York harassed them on one side, and New-Hampshire on the other. Finally, what was formerly called the N. Hampshire Grants that is, three tier of towns on the east side of Connecticut River, joined with Vermont, in order to help her obtain her state privileges. They at last agreed to give N. York thirty thousand dollars to relinquish their claim, and by that means Vermont obtained of Congress an admission into the union, on an equal footing with the original states.

In 1783, peace was declared between Great Britain and the United States, and the army was disbanded and returned home to their friends, without anything for their toils and sacrifices, but the consciousness of having "fought a good fight," and having won an invaluable inheritance for their posterity. The states laid heavy taxes, in order to defray their individual expenses in carrying on the war, which were burthensome to the people. But they finally paid into the state treasuries enough to redeem the paper they had issued, to pay the soldiers their bounty, which is more than could be said of the National Government, until after the poor soldiers had disposed of their hard-earnings for a tenth or twentieth part of its nominal value.

In 1785, I took a Captain's commission in the N. H. militia, signed by Meshick Ware, President; (for at that time there was no governor) and served eight years. I also served nine years as Selectman of Plainfield.

Chapter Eleven – Chelsea - 1797-1819

A New State and the War of 1812 (beginning).

In 1797, I moved to Chelsea, Vt.. and have lived here twenty one years last March, and helped pay the premium to New-York, in order to become a state -- and for a portion of the time we have been a state much opposition has been manifested by a part of our citizens, to-wards the general government, and in a very bad time, too, -- in a time of war, when we ought to have united as a band of brothers in the common cause of our country. But we were not alone in this evil. It has pervaded most of the New England states. I have lived to see four wars in our country, and the last was attended with difficulties harder to be surmounted than any of the other wars, by reason of the enmity, towards the General Government, of that portion of the people, who declared there was no cause of war with England, although she had taken between nine hundred and a thousand of our vessels, impressed some thousands of our citizens, and sent the Indians to massacre our defenceless inhabitants -- and not-withstanding the General Government had done every thing to effect an accommodation of their differences, and obtain redress for our grievances, without a resort to arms.

Chapter Twelve - Admonition to Future Generations (1819).

The War of 1812 (end)

I desire it may never be forgotten by my posterity, for whom I have written these memoirs, that there was once a time, when party spirit raged to an extent that threatened the destruction of those liberties, which I had some small share in establishing. I hope they will never forget, that when war was declared to maintain those liberties, there were men claiming all the wealth, talents and religion of the country, who, from party, or worse motives, held back their resources from Government, and did all in their power to keep those who were disposed to lend an assisting hand, from entering into their country's service. In the time of the Revolution we had a few such men among us, who set much by the British Government, and we drove them out of the country, or confined them at home, so that they could not meet in *Convention*, in the heart of the land, to plot against the government, and divide the Union. And I desire it may be remembered, that notwithstanding they boasted of their talents and religion, the Lord stood by us and put our enemies to flight in a marvellous manner, and wrought wonders for us as a nation: and we have the greatest reason to bless and praise his holy name, of any people on the earth. -- Let it be remembered, as a warning to future generations, of the dangerous effect of party spirit, when carried to excess, that a governor of Vermont, at a time when the enemy threatened a powerful invasion of our frontier towns, with the avowed intention of laying them in ruins, stood on the shores of the lake, discouraging our [valiant] freemen from going to the assistance of their brethren, by telling them they would be killed if they went over -- when he, and every other person of common sense, knew, that it would not be more than six hours before the enemy would be at Burlington, if he beat our men at Plattsburgh. But let it also, with gratitude, be remembered, that while the chief magistrate was thus employed, the gallant Col. Fassett encouraged and prevailed on them to go forward -- and they did go forward to participate in a glorious battle and victory, which preserved our towns from conflagration, and wiped the foul stain from the character of our state, which the conduct of this Governor would otherwise have brought upon it.

While the enemy were thus discomfited by land, we beheld the British fleet on the lake heaving in sight of the little squadron of the invincible Macdonough, who was on his knees, praying to his God; and He answered him by *fire*, as in former times -- and notwithstanding the enemies' superior force, they were obliged to strike -- and on that ever-memorable eleventh of September, the Lord discomfited their whole force, and returned them back from whence they came: so that we may see, that the *effectual, fervent prayer of a righteous man availeth much: and that the sacrifice of the wicked is an abomination to the Lord.* -- For the great men of a great state said, that it was unbecoming a moral and religious people to pray for the success of our arms, and that we must not fight the British, because they were "the Bulwark of our Religion." But I cannot but think, that they were deluded and blinded by party prejudices, and that the good hand of God was discernible at Baltimore, New-Orleans, and Plattsburgh, -- on Lake Erie, and Lake Champlain, and everywhere else that a *traitor* did not command. Had not the Lord been on our side, and fought our battles, we must have failed to maintain our liberties against so potent a foe from abroad, aided by so many of our misguided people at home -- and it becomes us as a people, (as I have before said,) to bless and praise his Holy name forever, that He caused us to overcome our powerful enemies in two wars for our independence, and that there seems now to be so happy a union taking place among ourselves -- that those of our fellow-citizens who have been thus deluded and deceived, are sensible of their errors, and appear ready to unite with all real friends of their country's honor and prosperity. -- And I pray God that this *bond of union* may continue to grow firmer and stronger, till every

American citizen will be of one heart and one mind, in a determination to support our Republican form of Government to the latest posterity. May we all remember the maxim of our illustrious Washington: **"United we stand; divided we fall."** -- When we reflect back to our Revolutionary war, and see how much blood and treasure were spent to gain our independence, shall we, after so long an experience of the advantages arising from so good a government, be any more deceived by internal or foreign enemies? Shall we contrast the mildness of our government, and the civil and religious liberty that we enjoy under it, with the bigotry and tyranny which prevails under the monarchies of Europe, and say we are willing to exchange the former for the latter? I dare say not. Then let me conjure my posterity to stand by this government of our choice, and never be deceived by political or ecclesiastical demagogues. Let the people keep the right and power of election; always in their own hands, and at their annual freemen's meetings be sure to choose men into office, who are true friends of a Republican Government. Let them encourage all the arts and sciences that are necessary in a Republic, and none others, -- and in this way they may perpetuate their liberties. -- But if they are ambitious to ape the follies, extravagance, and luxury of European countries, their freedom can have but a short duration. But, above all, let us as a nation dedicate ourselves to God, and pray that he would have us in his holy keeping, and so direct the councils of our nation, as may tend to preserve its free institutions, to the latest period of time; which is the ardent prayer of

David Perry

Chelsea, Vt. 1819

www.ingramcontent.com/pod-product-compliance
Lightning Source LLC
Chambersburg PA
CBHW031531040426
42445CB00009B/483